Taking Diabetes to School

by
Kim Gosselin

JayJo Books
Publishing Special Books for Special Kids®

Taking Diabetes to School
© 1998, 2004 JayJo Books
A Brand of The Guidance Group
1-800-999-6884
www.guidance-group.com

All rights reserved.

ISBN 10: 1-891383-28-0
ISBN 13: 978-1-891383-28-1
Library of Congress Control Number: 2004104429
Third Edition

Printed in the United States of America.

The opinions in this book are solely those of the author. Medical care is highly individualized and should never be altered without professional medical consultation.

Here's What Professionals Have to Say About
Taking Diabetes to School

Taking Diabetes to School is a superb children's book for kids with diabetes. This wonderfully illustrated book is written by a mother and her diabetic son, and will help children discuss their diabetes with their schoolmates and friends.

> Neil H. White, M.D.
> Associate Professor, Pediatrics
> Washington University School of Medicine
> St. Louis Children's Hospital

Kim Gosselin has done a marvelous job of explaining the complexities of diabetes to young students in "kid" language! A **"MUST HAVE"** for every elementary school library!

> Connie Madigan, R.N., B.S.N.
> Elementary School Nurse

Taking Diabetes to School fills the enormous need of educating classmates of a child with diabetes. **A BARGAIN AT ANY PRICE!**

> Libby O'Connor, M.S.N., R.N., C.D.E.
> Manager, Diabetes Services
> Barnes Hospital, St. Louis, MO

Taking Diabetes to School offers sensitive insight into the day-to-day "school life" of a child with a chronic illness. Kim Gosselin has done an excellent job of conveying the message that a child with diabetes can live a happy, normal life! The "real" Jayson is a wonderful, happy, and talented little boy who is an inspiration to all who know and love him.

> Pat Thomas, M. Ed.
> Kindergarten teacher, living with diabetes herself

More of What Professionals Have to Say About
Taking Diabetes to School

As a health care professional and mother, I found Taking Diabetes to School to be an insightful, poignant look into the school day of a child living with diabetes. **INSPIRATIONAL!!**

> **Lynn Schratz, R.N., B.S.N.**
> **Clinical Research Specialist**
> **St. Louis University Hospital**

Taking Diabetes to School is an easy-to-understand book written from the diabetic child's perspective. It **SUPERBLY** fills the very important need of educating teachers as well as classmates of young children living with diabetes.

> **Anne Fitz, R.N., M.S.N.**
> **St. Louis Children's Hospital**

An **EXCELLENT** idea! Does a wonderful job of educating kids with or without diabetes, and the illustrations are delightful!

> **Jeanne Bubb, A.C.S.W., M.S.W.**
> **Diabetes Team Social Worker**
> **St. Louis Children's Hospital**

Taking Diabetes to School was born out of necessity. It is education in the finest form and would have helped my own son tremendously when he was younger.

> **Jackie Smith, former NFL football player and**
> **father of a college student living with diabetes**
> **Member of the NFL Hall of Fame**

Acknowledgements

*With many thanks and true understanding
to all families living with diabetes*

Preface

On February 29, 1992, my son Jayson was diagnosed with type 1 (insulin dependent) diabetes. It was just nine days after he celebrated his sixth birthday. Adjustments at home fell into place rather quickly. Injections, finger-pricks, and eating the proper foods were suddenly part of our regular routine. Attending school, however, presented a whole new set of frustrations and concerns. How could I expect Jayson's young classmates, or even his teachers, to understand the complexities of diabetes?

Searching for a simple picture book on the topic of school and diabetes proved futile. I was appalled to find none available, and soon felt compelled to write one myself. Thus, Taking Diabetes to School was born! Since I began reading this little book to my son's classes, most of his "problems" regarding school and diabetes have been solved. His classmates have shown a new respect and admiration for Jayson. The children I have met delighted in the learning process and exhibited understanding and acceptance.

Taking Diabetes to School was designed to be read aloud in the child's classroom. Try to make it a fun event, and be prepared for some very bright questions from the other students. Involve your own child by asking him (or her) to pass out sugar-free treats when the story is finished. Of course, get permission from the teacher first.

Please feel free to write me in care of the publisher, as I welcome your comments and suggestions. My heart goes out to each and every one of you, and I yearn for the day when children are no longer Taking Diabetes to School.

Kim Gosselin

*To my very special son Jayson,
whose courage and zest for life continue to
inspire me each and every day.*

Hello, boys and girls! My name is Jayson, and I'm a kid living with diabetes. Having diabetes means the part of my body called the pancreas doesn't make enough insulin anymore. Because of this, I get too much sugar in my blood. Insulin is something special our bodies make to help turn sugar into energy. This sugar comes from the foods we eat.

Everyone has a pancreas, but not everyone gets diabetes.

Doctors and nurses don't know how or why I have diabetes. I didn't do anything wrong (like eating too many sweets), and it's nobody's fault! Doctors and nurses do know you can't catch diabetes from me. It's okay to play with me and be my friend.

I can't give you diabetes.

Has anyone noticed the special bracelet I always wear? Bracelets aren't just for girls—mine is really awesome! On the back it says that I have diabetes. It also has a phone number to call in case of emergency (like if my blood sugar dropped too low, or if I had an accident). The people who answer the phone can tell the caller about diabetes and how to take special care of me.

I never take my bracelet off. Someday it could save my life.

Because I have diabetes, it's important for me to eat healthy foods at about the same time each day. I follow a meal plan that I have written down. My meal plan works together with my insulin to help me stay healthy and feel my best. It's a kind of "diet" that's good for anyone!

When you see me eating healthy snacks in class, it's because I'm following my meal plan.

To help keep my blood sugar in good control, I use a small computer called a meter. It does a test that tells me how much sugar is in my blood. The test helps my doctors and nurses decide how much insulin my body needs.

When you see me leave the classroom, I might be going to visit the school nurse. She helps me do my blood test. Teachers can help too! When I'm at home, I usually do it myself.

The test takes me only a few seconds, and it doesn't even hurt.

One way for my body to get the insulin it needs is in a shot. Usually I get two or more shots each day. When I first went to the hospital, everyone did a great job of teaching me and my family about diabetes. We learned how to give shots at home. They don't hurt very much, and I can even do it myself (with help from my family, of course).

Because I get shots of insulin every day, it's no big deal. It's just something I do, like eating breakfast or brushing my teeth.

Some kids, like my friend Laci, wear an insulin pump. It's a small computer with buttons, and it looks like the pager my dad wears on his belt. It's really cool! The pump gives Laci a small amount of insulin all day, every day. When she eats carbohydrates, which are foods that turn into sugar quickly, she pushes a special button on her pump to get extra insulin.

Her doctors and nurses taught Laci and her family how to count the number of carbohydrates in her food and figure out how much extra insulin she needs. There was a lot to learn before Laci was allowed to use a pump.

Someday, I might wear an insulin pump, but I'm not ready yet. My doctors and nurses said it's a big decision!

If I exercise a lot or don't have enough food in my body to balance my insulin, my blood sugar might drop too low. Laci has to be especially careful of "lows," because her body is getting insulin from her pump all the time.

When I'm "low," I might act differently than I normally do. I might get shaky, hungry, or sleepy. At times, I might feel mean, angry, or confused. Please tell the teacher if you see me act this way. I need to eat or drink something with sugar in it **fast** when I'm feeling low. Orange juice or regular soda works great.

After a few minutes, I'll be back to my old self again!

Like most kids, I love to play at recess and take part in gym class. I bet you do too! Unless I've just eaten a meal, it's probably best for me to have an extra snack before doing lots of exercise. Then I'm sure to have plenty of energy to play and have fun.

Sometimes, Laci has to adjust her amount of insulin when she exercises. During heavy exercise, she doesn't need as much insulin as at other times.

Diabetes doesn't stop Laci or me from doing anything other kids do!

I hope someday there will be a cure, so Laci and I won't have to live with diabetes anymore! Important people are working hard to find a cure for diabetes every day. Until then, please don't treat me like I'm someone different because I have diabetes. After all, nobody is perfect!

We're just Jayson and Laci—kids living with diabetes, but a lot like you in every other way!

Let's Take The Diabetes Kids' Quiz!

1. What is insulin?
    Something special our bodies make to help turn the sugar in our foods into energy.

2. What part of my body doesn't make enough insulin anymore?
    The pancreas.

3. Where in my body is the pancreas found?
    Near my stomach.

4. Does someone get diabetes from eating too many sweets?
    No!

5. Can you catch diabetes from me or anyone else?
    No, so it's okay to play with me and be my friend.

6. Since my body doesn't make enough insulin anymore, how do I get the insulin my body needs?
    I get my insulin in a shot, usually two or more each day. Laci gets her insulin through an insulin pump that she wears every day.

7. Does getting your insulin shots hurt?
Not very much at all...I can even do it myself (with help from my family, my nurse, or my doctor, of course!).

8. What is a meal plan?
A meal plan is eating healthy foods at about the same time each day. It's important for me to stay on my meal plan. You may even see me eating snacks in class!

9. What is a meter?
It's a small computer that tells me how much sugar is in my blood. My meter helps me know if I need to eat an extra snack or how much insulin my body needs.

10. What happens if my blood test tells me my blood sugar is too low?
Then I need to eat or drink something with sugar in it FAST. Orange juice or regular soda works great!

Great job! Thanks for taking the Diabetes Kids' Quiz
and learning more about diabetes!

Ten Tips For Teachers

1. **EVERY CHILD LIVING WITH DIABETES IS DIFFERENT.**
   Every child living with diabetes may have different symptoms of "low" blood sugar. Although many of the symptoms may be similar, they will not always be the same. Situations that can affect your student's blood sugar are: insulin, food intake, exercise, illness, stress, and/or any changes in routine. Soon you will get to know your own student's unique individuality and their typical reactions to "low" blood sugar. Remember to pay especially close attention to possible "lows" if your student wears an insulin pump.

2. **DON'T DRAW UNNECESSARY ATTENTION TO YOUR STUDENT'S CONDITION.**
   Since your student living with diabetes may have to eat snacks periodically in the classroom, allow the whole class to have a snack at the necessary time. This tells the student who MUST have a snack that it's okay to eat when he or she needs to, without singling the student out as being "different." In addition to your student's designated snack time, remember that he or she MUST eat whenever the student feels "low." This is imperative, especially if the student is unable to have their blood sugar checked first by the school nurse. This is NOT a choice for the child living with diabetes, but a necessity!

3. **PROVIDE INCONSPICUOUS AND GENTLE REMINDERS.**
   Pay close attention to your student's regular snack time. Not all children (especially the very young) can tell time, or are going to remember their snack time. If you haven't noticed him/her eating, pass the student a note or work out a special "password" between the two of you to remind him/her of their snack time.

4. **DO NOT PUT A "LABEL" ON THE STUDENT LIVING WITH DIABETES.**
   Never single out a child living with diabetes as the "diabetic" kid. First and foremost, the child living with diabetes needs and wants to feel unique and special, just like every other student.

5. **DO NOT SYMPATHIZE; EMPATHIZE.**
   A child with diabetes does not want or need your sympathy. These children need understanding, acceptance, and support. Educate yourself in every way possible regarding type 1 diabetes. Learn how it may affect them and have compassion for how they must live their lives every day.

6. **ALWAYS BE PREPARED.**
Always carry a quick and portable snack WHENEVER you and your student living with diabetes leave the classroom or the school grounds. This is especially important during fire drills, earthquake drills, field trips, special presentations, and/or assemblies. A small can of juice together with crackers may work best.

7. **USE THE BUDDY SYSTEM.**
If your student living with diabetes tells you he or she feels "low" and needs to see the nurse, ALWAYS send a "buddy" (someone who won't object) with the student. In rare instances, the child's blood sugar may be so "low" that he/she may become disoriented and not make it to the nurse's office if left alone. Again, this is the rare extreme, but it does happen.

8. **ALLOW UNRESTRICTED BATHROOM BREAKS.**
When given the opportunity, let the child living with diabetes know that it's okay to go to the bathroom WHENEVER necessary. If their blood sugar is running "high," their body's natural response is to eliminate the extra glucose by using the bathroom.

9. **BE PATIENT.**
Be patient if the student living with diabetes has minor problems with organization. "High" and/or "low" blood sugar levels may make it difficult for the student to concentrate at times. You may have to repeat some things, especially if he/she has been to the nurse's office during class time.

10. **KEEP THE LINES OF COMMUNICATION OPEN.**
Always work together with the student, caregivers, school nurse, and other educators as a team player. If there is a special school party or occasion where "treats" will be served, let the family know in advance, if possible. This allows the family to discuss the options with the child, so that he or she can make responsible choices. Often, "treats" can be worked into the child's regular meal plan.

The Special Kids in School® series is designed to be read in the classroom in order to normalize and provide understanding of conditions. The books are designed to show the chronically ill child's peers that he/she is just like them but with special challenges that he/she faces with courage and fortitude every day. When children understand conditions such as childhood diabetes, asthma, autism, allergies, A.D.H.D., and other illnesses, they lose their fear, better understand their classmate, and embrace him/her as a friend.

The Special Kids in School® series titles include:

Taking A.D.H.D. to School

Taking Arthritis to School

Taking Asthma to School

Taking Autism to School

Taking Cancer to School

Taking Cerebral Palsy to School

Taking Cystic Fibrosis to School

Taking Depression to School

Taking Diabetes to School

Taking Down Syndrome to School

Taking Dyslexia to School

Taking Food Allergies to School

Taking Hearing Impairment to School

Taking Seizure Disorders to School

Taking Speech Disorders to School

Taking Tourette Syndrome to School

Taking Visual Impairment to School

Taking Weight Problems to School

To order additional copies of this book or inquire about our quantity discounts for schools, hospitals, and affiliated organizations, contact us at 1-800-999-6884.